God's Plan for Humanity:

Purpose, Provision & Prosperity

BY
TONYA HAUGABROOK

A Goshen Publishers Book

ISBN: 978-1-7342639-3-0

Library of Congress Cataloging-in-Publication Data

Published in 2020 by:
GOSHEN PUBLISHERS LLC
P.O. Box 1562
Stephens City, Virginia, USA
www.GoshenPublishers.com

Our books may be purchased in bulk for promotional, educational, or business use. For inquiries please contact the publisher via email: Agents@GoshenPublishers.com.

Published in 2004 by The Right Start Publishers. Reprinted by Nehemiah's Vision in 2006.

Third Edition 2020

Cover designed by Goshen Publishers LLC

Printed in the United States of America

All Scriptures are quoted from the King James translation of the Bible unless otherwise noted. All term definitions are retrieved from dictionary.com unless otherwise noted.

10 9 8 7 6 5 4 3

God's Plan for Humanity:

Purpose, Provision & Prosperity

DEDICATION

I dedicate this book to all who are near and dear to my heart:

My Lord and Savior, Jesus Christ, who is all that I am or ever hope to be. All the glory belongs to Him;

My children, the three most loving and supportive kids a mother could ask for;

My parents, the late Min. Diane Johnson and Joseph Haugabrook, Sr., who taught me to be strong and to believe in my dreams;

My siblings, with whom I share unconditional love and boundless friendship;

My many friends who give me hope and encouragement, and pray for me; and

My Pastors who, throughout the years, have always guided me in the spirit of Christ.

INTRODUCTION

I believe that God allows us to prevail over life's challenges to be witnesses to others. This book is my short but powerful testimony of realizing that God has a plan for my life and yours.

Life is not always a bed of roses but when you realize that God's plan for you includes a purpose, provision, and prosperity, you then understand that the good, the bad, and the ugly will work for your good.

> Likewise the Spirit also helpeth our infirmities: for we know not what we should pray for as we ought: but the Spirit itself
>
> maketh intercession for us with groanings which cannot be uttered.
>
> And he that searcheth the hearts knoweth what is the mind of the Spirit, because he maketh intercession for the saints according to the will of God.
>
> And we know that all things work together for good to them that love God, to them who are the called according to his purpose.
>
> For whom he did foreknow, he also did predestinate to be conformed to the image of his Son, that he might be the firstborn among many brethren.

Moreover whom he did predestinate, them he also called: and whom he called, them he also justified: and whom he justified, them he also glorified.

What shall we then say to these things? If God be for us, who can be against us?

Romans 8:26-31

CONTENTS

1.   GOD'S PURPOSE FOR HUMANITY

PURPOSE: the reason for which something exists or is done, made, used, etc.

Have you ever wondered why God created humanity? It was for a purpose.

> *So God created man in His own image, in the image of God created He him; male and female created He them.*
>
> *And God blessed them, and God said unto them, "Be fruitful and multiply, and replenish the earth, and subdue it; and have dominion over the fish of the sea, and over the fowl of the air, and over every living thing that moveth upon the earth."*
>
> Genesis 1:27-28

When looking closely at Genesis 1:27-28 it is clear that God had a purpose for humanity when He created man (male and female). When God created man in his own image His intent was to create a freewill being that was a reflection of His character. When He told them to be fruitful and multiply, He was establishing a world of individuals with whom He could have perfect fellowship. When He told them to subdue the earth and have dominion over the animals, He had established them to reign on earth like he reigns in heaven.

God had the perfect plan for man, but Adam's disobedience disrupted that plan. (Read about The Fall in Genesis 3.) That is why Romans 5:19 is a verse that every man and woman should never forget.

> "For as by one man's disobedience many were made sinners, so by the obedience of One shall many be made righteous."

Knowing that sinners could not have fellowship with Him or partake of His glory, God set a plan in motion after Adam's disobedience to ensure that all humanity could partake of His original purpose for man. It is so wonderful to know that despite our disobedience God loves us so much that He would go to such great lengths to ensure that we will one day again be like Him.

How great is the love the Father has lavished on us, that we should be called children of God! And that is what we are!

The reason the world does not know us is that it did not know Him.

Behold, what manner of love the Father hath bestowed upon us, that we should be called the sons of God: therefore the world knoweth us not, because it knew him not.

Beloved, now are we the sons of God, and it doth not yet appear what we shall be: but we know that, when he shall appear, we shall be like him; for we shall see him as he is.

And every man that hath this hope in him purifieth himself, even as he is pure.

1 John 3:1-3

God is faithful and he never changes. If He never changes that means His ways and intents never change. God still wants us to be a reflection of His character and to reign in this earthly realm, and he still wants to have fellowship with us.

1.1 GOD'S PURPOSE— HAVE DOMINION

DOMINION: the power or right of governing and controlling; sovereign authority

God's intent for man (man male and man female) was to be dominant over all His other creations. Genesis 1:28 clearly states the dominionship that God had established for humanity. Yet, today we live in a world where many Christians fear everything, even their own shadows.

God never meant for man to live in fear. Even the Word tells us that fear carries with it torment. The torment of wondering *Will I make it? Can I make it? What happens when I make it?* all lead to double-minded thinking. It is imperative to know that God has told us in James 1:8 that a double-minded man should not expect anything from Him.

That is exactly what the enemy wants for your life, for you to receive nothing from God so that he can send his curses of trickery that will move you further from the will of God.

The enemy wants you to feel like you are defeated, not dominant. That is why you must remember Romans 8:37. There is nothing that satan can throw at you that God has not already made you an overcomer through Christ's sacrifice on the cross.

> *Nay, in all these things we are more than conquerors through him that loved us.*

> Romans 8:37

1.2 GOD'S PURPOSE— REFLECT HIS CHARACTER

CHARACTER: the aggregate of features and traits that form the individual nature of some person or thing

What is the character (reflection of God) that others should see in you, in me, and all Christians?

1.2.1 Overcomers

When we reflect God's character, we are overcomers.

> *I have written unto you, fathers, because ye have known him that is from the beginning. I have written unto you, young men, because ye are strong, and the word of God abideth in you, and ye have overcome the wicked one.*

1 John 2:14

> *Ye are of God, little children, and have overcome them: because greater is he that is in you, than he that is in the world.*

1 John 4:4

> *For whatsoever is born of God overcometh the world: and this is the victory that overcometh the world, even our faith. Who is he that overcometh the world, but he that believeth that Jesus is the Son of God?*

1 John 5:4-5

1.2.2 Fruit of the Spirit

When we reflect God's character, we display what Galatians 5:22-23 teaches us as the "fruit of the Spirit."

> *But the fruit of the Spirit is love, joy, peace, longsuffering, gentleness, goodness, faith, meekness, temperance: against such there is no law*

LOVE:
A deep, intense affection shown to others with no thought of reward

> *No man hath seen God at any time. If we love one another, God dwelleth in us, and his love is perfected in us.*

> *1 John 4:12*

JOY:
Continual happiness and delight

> *These things have I spoken unto you, that my joy might remain in you, and that your joy might be full.*

> *John 15:11*

PEACE:
Harmony and quietness

Thou wilt keep him in perfect peace, whose mind is stayed on thee: because he trusteth in thee.

Isaiah 26:3

LONGSUFFERING:
The patient endurance of hardship

Now the God of patience and consolation grant you to be likeminded one toward another according to Christ Jesus

Romans 15:5

GENTLENESS:
Calmness

To speak evil of no man, to be no brawlers, but gentle, shewing all meekness unto all men.

Titus 3:2

GOODNESS:
Integrity; Honesty

I would have lost heart, unless I had believed that I would see the goodness of the Lord in the land of the living.

Psalm 27:13

FAITH:
Reliance; Assurance

Now faith is the substance of things hoped for, the evidence of things not seen.

Hebrews 11:1

MEEKNESS:
Submissiveness; Humbleness

Blessed are the meek: for they shall inherit the earth.

Matthew 5:5

TEMPERANCE:
Self-Control

Wherefore, my beloved brethren, let every man be swift to hear, slow to speak, slow to wrath:

James 1:19

As you can see, God's Word lets us know how critical these characteristics are in pleasing God in our Christian walk.

1.2.3 GOD'S PURPOSE—
TO FELLOWSHIP

FELLOWSHIP: *friendly relationship; companionship*

God never intended for us to serve Him as slaves. God's purpose for us was to have the fellowship that a father has with his children. While man's ideology a of father and child relationship has changed over the years, God's has not. The infallible Word of God lets us know that God does not change. Regardless of the circumstance, He remains the same.

So, when God tells us that we are His children, He is letting us know that the fellowship He purposed for us was for Him to be our provider and protector. That has always been God's purpose for humanity. God never intended for us to work from sunup to sundown in order to survive. He never meant for us to have to fight the elements of this world to get a single meal. He never meant for us to be fearful in His presence.

God's purpose for humanity has always been to have the perfect father and child fellowship. In turn, we would be so overwhelmed with love and admiration for God that praising Him would be first nature.

Does praising God come naturally to you? If so, you probably have the type of relationship He desires with you.

2.   GOD'S PROVISION FOR HUMANITY

PROVISION: the providing or supplying of something, especially of food or other necessities

2.1 GOD'S PROVISION—TO PROVIDE

But my God shall supply all your need according to his riches in glory by Christ Jesus.

Philippians 4:19

It is not enough for a father to just say to his children that he loves them, but that love will always manifest itself in some type of actions or deeds. For example, a father that loves his children sees the need for his children to live in a decent home, have balanced meals and suitable clothing, and will therefore work diligently and honestly to provide those things. This is the same way God desires to provide for us.

It was never God's intent that man would have to go out into what we now call the "rat race" in order to obtain food to eat or shelter from the outside elements. God created man so He knew what was required for man to live in perfect fellowship with

Him, not just to survive. God always intended to provide the needs for man for that was His original provision for humanity, to provide man's every need.

Through the world of medical science, God has allowed His children to learn of the physical implications of worrying and living in fear to help us to see that those results are contrary to His promise of physical health. That is not to say we will never encounter any physical sickness or ailment, but we do not have to live a lifestyle that constantly invites sicknesses and ailments into our lives simply because we fail to trust God. He promises us long life with satisfaction; we just only need to position ourselves to receive it. We only need to walk in the Spirit.

> *My son, forget not my law; but let thine heart keep my commandments:*
>
> *For length of days, and long life, and peace, shall they add to thee.*
>
> *Let not mercy and truth forsake thee: bind them about thy neck; write them upon the table of thine heart:*
>
> *So shalt thou find favour and good understanding in the sight of God and man. Trust in the LORD with all thine heart; and lean not unto thine own understanding.*
>
> *In all thy ways acknowledge him, and he shall direct thy paths.*

Be not wise in thine own eyes: fear the LORD, and depart from evil.

It shall be health to thy navel, and marrow to thy bones.

Proverbs 3:1-8

And ye shall serve the LORD your God, and he shall bless thy bread, and thy water; and I will take sickness away from the midst of thee.

Exodus 23:25

Because thou hast made the LORD, which is my refuge, even the most High, thy habitation;

There shall no evil befall thee, neither shall any plague come nigh thy dwelling.

For he shall give his angels charge over thee, to keep thee in all thy ways.

They shall bear thee up in their hands, lest thou dash thy foot against a stone.

Thou shalt tread upon the lion and adder: the young lion and the dragon shalt thou trample under feet.

Because he hath set his love upon me, therefore will I deliver him: I will set him on high, because he hath known my name.

He shall call upon me, and I will answer him:
I will be with him in trouble; I will deliver him,
and honour him.

With long life will I satisfy him, and shew him
my salvation.

Psalm 91:9-16

As children of God we have a promise that God will provide all our needs. He wants us to trust and believe that there is no need too big or too small for Him.

The Message version of the Bible, describes it this way:

> *Honor God with everything you own; give him the first and the best. Your barns will burst, your wine vats will brim over. But don't, dear friend, resent God's discipline; don't sulk under his loving correction. It's the child he loves that God corrects; a father's delight is behind all this.*

Psalm 91:9-16, MSG

You see, God's desire is for us to live long but, more importantly, to live well. The only way to get that promised provision from Him is to live in fellowship with Him.

2.2 GOD'S PROVISION—PROTECTION

PROTECTION: *defend or guard from attack, invasion, loss, annoyance, insult, etc.; cover or shield from injury or danger*

God has always desired to protect man. When he placed man in the midst of the Garden of Eden, He gave instruction as to which plants and trees were good for food and which one that would cause harm. Although Adam and Eve did not see it then, God was trying to protect them.

Even after they had eaten and realized they were naked, God made clothes for them to cover their nakedness. Then, to show His unfailing love, to protect them He drove them out of the Garden of Eden so that man would not live forever in a sinful state.

When I first read about Adam and Eve, I wondered why God would not let them stay in the Garden. I now realize that God was trying to protect man from an eternal life of sin. God put into motion the plan to restore man to the original fellowship He had purposed for him.

We see an example of God's protection when the children of Israel were leaving Egypt. Pharaoh's heart was hardened against them to the point that he decided to send his fastest chariots and strongest army out to destroy them. Pharaoh did not understand he was not battling the Israelites, but God almighty Himself. Pharaoh just knew he would catch them at the banks of the Red Sea, but JEHOVAH NISSI (God our Banner) had already made provisions for His children to cross over that sea on dry land. Pharaoh's army, on the other hand, was overtaken by waters and perished. (Read that story in Exodus 14.)

There is another example when Satan went to God to ask permission to try Job (Job 1:6-12). We see how God gave permission for satan to attack Job in the natural, but satan could not harm his soul. Again, we see how God made provisions so that link that allowed Job to fellowship with God was protected.

Even today, God's hand of protection surrounds us and keeps satan and his angels from killing our souls.

2.3 GOD'S PROVISION—RECONCILIATION

RECONCILIATION: *to bring into agreement or harmony; make compatible or consistent*

When we repent of our sins and accept Christ as our Lord and Savior, we are then reconciled to Christ through the forgiveness of our sins. God blots out our sin thereby making us right in His eyes.

Have you accepted Christ yet? If not, all you have to do is pray according to Romans 10:9-10:

That if thou shalt confess with thy mouth the Lord Jesus, and shalt believe in thine heart that God hath raised him from the dead, thou shalt be saved.

For with the heart man believeth unto righteousness; and with the mouth confession is made unto salvation.

I would like to pray the prayer of salvation with you now:

Dear Lord Jesus, I know that I am a sinner, and I ask for Your forgiveness. I believe You died for my sins and rose from the dead. I turn from my sins and invite You to come into my heart and life. I want to trust and follow You as my Lord and Savior. Amen.

As you see, positioning yourself to receive God's provisions are neither hard nor complicated.

Once saved, we then become ambassadors for Christ. An ambassador is an official representative of a country to another country. In John 14:3, Jesus said He was going away to prepare a place for us so we can be with Him. As ambassadors for the Kingdom of God we are compelled to encourage others to accept Christ as their Lord and Savior and be reconciled to God, and one day be able to enjoy life in the beautiful kingdom God has prepared for His obedient children.

And all things are of God, who hath reconciled us to Himself by Jesus Christ and hath given to us the ministry of reconciliation,

to wit, that God was in Christ, reconciling the world unto Himself, not imputing their trespasses unto them, and hath committed unto us the Word of reconciliation.

Now then we are ambassadors for Christ, as though God were beseeching you by us: we pray you on Christ's stead, be ye reconciled to God.

For He hath made Him who knew no sin to be sin for us, that we might be made the righteousness of God in Him.

2 Corinthians 5:18-21

I am sure that about now you are ready to start shouting but hold on a few minutes while we look at God's prosperity for humanity.

3.   GOD'S PROSPERITY FOR HUMANITY

PROSPERITY: *a successful, flourishing, or thriving condition, especially in financial respects; good fortune*

3.1 GOD'S PROSPERITY—SPIRITUALLY

Beloved, I wish above all things that thou mayest prosper and be in health, even as thy soul prospereth.

3 John 1:2

While it is acceptable to gain material wealth, you should never neglect your true-life purpose: to worship and praise God. Through worship and praise you establish the fellowship that God first designed and desired when He created man.

WORSHIP: *reverent honor and homage paid to God or a sacred personage, or to any object regarded as sacred*

PRAISE: *the act of expressing approval or admiration; commendation; laudation.*

Dedicating time to worship and praise God means you will spend more time walking in the spirit because God is a spirit and the Word of God says you can only worship God in the Spirit.

> But the hour cometh, and now is, when the true worshippers shall worship the Father in spirit and in truth: for the Father seeketh such to worship him.

> God is a Spirit: and they that worship him must worship him in spirit and in truth.

> John 4:23-24

As you prosper spiritually, you will have a stronger relationship and connection to God. That relationship and connection will cause you to increase in love, compassion, gratitude, generosity, and kindness. But you can only increase in those areas by seeking God first.

> And He will give you all you need from day to day if you live for Him and make the Kingdom of God your primary concern.

> Matthew 6:33

3.2 GOD'S PROSPERITY—PHYSICALLY

God's Word shows the connection between our spiritual and physical prosperity. As you grow in the spirit, your trust in God grows to the point that you acknowledge God in every aspect of your life — from guidance when purchasing a home to the best route to take when going to work. You will take nothing for granted but will put God first in all you do.

When you are assured that God is leading the way, you have confidence that no matter what you may encounter in between the time you make your request known to God and God's appointed time for arrival or manifestation, that everything is working out for your good; thus, closing the door to fear and worrying.

3.3   GOD'S PROSPERITY—MATERIALLY

Your spiritual prosperity is not only connected to your physical prosperity, but also your material prosperity.

The Bible is full of God's promises to those that obey His Word. What is so loving about God is that He gives us incentives to live holy. Imagine that! The God of the universe who is holy giving incentives to you and me — sinful man — to live holy so He can bless us.

How does this show His love for you? It's because God does not need or want for anything. The earth and all its fullness belong to Him. He controls the elements of the air, heals every sickness and disease, and speaks anything into existence. In other words, God does not need you or me to exist. We need Him.

Without God you are destined to a life of misery and pain. Yet, despite all your fallacies and shortcomings, God continues to show you grace and mercy and blesses you beyond what you deserve. Now if that is not love, what is?

> *For when we were yet without strength, in due time Christ died for the ungodly.*
>
> *For scarcely for a righteous man will one die: yet peradventure for a good man some would even dare to die.*
>
> *But God commendeth his love toward us, in that, while we were yet sinners, Christ died for us.*
>
> Romans 5:6-8

> *And it shall come to pass, if thou shalt hearken diligently unto the voice of the LORD thy God, to observe and to do all his commandments which I command thee this day, that the LORD thy God will set thee on high above all nations of the earth:*
>
> *And all these blessings shall come on thee, and overtake thee, if thou shalt hearken unto the voice of the LORD thy God.*
>
> *Blessed shalt thou be in the city, and blessed shalt thou be in the field.*
>
> *Blessed shall be the fruit of thy body, and the fruit of thy ground, and the fruit of thy*

cattle, the increase of thy kine, and the flocks of thy sheep.

Blessed shall be thy basket and thy store. Blessed shalt thou be when thou comest in, and blessed shalt thou be when thou goest out.

The LORD shall cause thine enemies that rise up against thee to be smitten before thy face: they shall come out against thee one way, and flee before thee seven ways.

The LORD shall command the blessing upon thee in thy storehouses, and in all that thou settest thine hand unto; and he shall bless thee in the land which the LORD thy God giveth thee.

Deuteronomy 28:1-8

The blessing of the LORD, it maketh rich, and he addeth no sorrow with it.

Proverbs 10:22

To fully understand God's desire to prosper us, we must always remember God's original purpose for man: to love and share fellowship with us as a father does his children.

When you were first born, you knew nothing of your father. Even if you were to look at the many baby pictures you have of the two of you together, you did not know your father's purpose in your life at that time. But as you grew and spent more time with your father it became evident of the characteristics of a true father: one who loves unconditionally, provides unselfishly, and protects fearlessly.

That is the type of quality time God desires to spend with you. He wants you to know Him so well that you know your spiritual, physical, and material prosperity all come from Him.

JEHOVAH JIREH —
He will provide for your needs.

> *And Abraham took the wood of the burnt offering, and laid it upon Isaac his son; and he took the fire in his hand, and a knife; and they went both of them together.*
>
> *And Isaac spake unto Abraham his father, and said, My father: and he said, Here am I, my son. And he said, Behold the fire and the wood: but where is the lamb for a burnt offering?*
>
> *And Abraham said, My son, God will provide himself a lamb for a burnt offering: so they went both of them together.*
>
> *And they came to the place which God had told him of; and Abraham built an altar there, and laid the wood in order, and bound Isaac his son, and laid him on the altar upon the wood.*

And Abraham stretched forth his hand, and took the knife to slay his son.

And the angel of the LORD called unto him out of heaven, and said, Abraham, Abraham: and he said, Here am I.

And he said, Lay not thine hand upon the lad, neither do thou any thing unto him: for now I know that thou fearest God, seeing thou hast not withheld thy son, thine only son from me.

And Abraham lifted up his eyes, and looked, and behold behind him a ram caught in a thicket by his horns: and Abraham went and took the ram, and offered him up for a burnt offering in the stead of his son.

And Abraham called the name of that place Jehovahjireh: as it is said to this day, In the mount of the LORD it shall be seen.

Genesis 22:6-14

JEHOVAH ROPHE —
He is your healer.

And he cried unto the LORD; and the LORD shewed him a tree, which when he had cast into the waters, the waters were made sweet: there he made for them a statute and an ordinance, and there he proved them,

And said, If thou wilt diligently hearken to the voice of the LORD thy God, and wilt do that which is right in his sight, and wilt give ear to his commandments, and keep all his statutes, I will put none of these diseases upon thee, which I have brought upon the Egyptians: for I am the LORD that healeth thee.

Exodus 15:25-26

JEHOVAH TSIDKENU —
He is our righteousness.

Behold, the days come, saith the Lord, that I will raise unto David a righteous Branch, and a King shall reign and prosper, and shall execute judgment and justice in the earth.

In his days Judah shall be saved, and Israel shall dwell safely: and this is his name whereby he shall be called, The Lord Our Righteousness.

Jeremiah 23:5-6

I know there is no way after reading this you can't help but stop to give God a shout of praise!

4.   GOD'S PLAN FOR HUMANITY

Therefore if any man be in Christ, he is a new creature: old things are passed away; behold, all things are become new.

And all things are of God, who hath reconciled us to himself by Jesus Christ, and hath given to us the ministry of reconciliation;

To wit, that God was in Christ, reconciling the world unto himself, not imputing their trespasses unto them; and hath committed unto us the word of reconciliation.

2 Corinthians 5:17-19

In summary, understanding God's purpose, provision and prosperity for humanity assures us that God never gave up on His original plan to fellowship, provide for, and prosper you. Even before Adam and Eve realized the implications of their disobedience, God put into action the plan to restore and reconcile man unto himself.

Knowing that God's plan for you has not changed should encourage you to position yourself to receive the fullness of God's promises.

In closing, I leave you with the following Scriptures to help you as you live just as God has planned for you: on purpose, with provision, and in prosperity.

> But ye are a chosen generation, a royal priesthood, an holy nation, a peculiar people; that ye should shew forth the praises of him who hath called you out of darkness into his marvelous light;
>
> Which in time past were not a people, but are now the people of God: which had not obtained mercy, but now have obtained mercy.

1 Peter 2:9-10

> For thou, O God, hast heard my vows: thou hast given me the heritage of those that fear thy name.

Psalm 61:5

> No weapon that is formed against thee shall prosper; and every tongue that shall rise against thee in judgment thou shalt condemn. This is the heritage of the servants of the LORD, and their righteousness is of me, saith the LORD.

Isaiah 54:17

> These things I have spoken unto you, that in me ye might have peace. In the world ye shall

have tribulation: but be of good cheer; I have overcome the world.

John 16:33

To contact Author Tonya Haugabrook or to find other books by her, visit GoshenPublishers.com/Tonya-Haugabrook.

God bless you.

www.ingramcontent.com/pod-product-compliance
Lightning Source LLC
Chambersburg PA
CBHW071753020426
42331CB00008B/2305